COMPLETE GUIDE TO HEDGEHOG FARMING

Expert Tips, Breeding Techniques, Care Strategies, And Profitable Business Insights For Successful Breeding

GIOVANNI MALAKAI

DISCLAIMER

This book's content is solely intended for informational and educational purposes. The author and publisher of this book make no express or implied representations or warranties of any kind regarding the completeness, accuracy, reliability, suitability, or availability of the information, products, services, or related graphics contained in it, even though every effort has been made to ensure their accuracy and dependability. You consequently absolutely assume all risk associated with any reliance you may have on such material.

The author's own experiences and studies serve as the foundation for the techniques and procedures covered in this book. They might not be appropriate for every circumstance or person. Before putting any advice or recommendations from this book into practice, readers should use their own discretion and take into account their unique situation. Consulting with qualified professionals who specialize in veterinary care and animal management is always a good idea. Any direct, indirect, incidental or consequential damages resulting from using or relying on the material in this book are disclaimed by the author and publisher. Any decisions made by the reader based on the information presented herein are at their own risk.

TABLE OF CONTENTS

ABOUT THE BOOK

The "Complete Guide to Hedgehog Farming" is an essential tool for anyone thinking about getting into the fascinating field of hedgehog farming or for those who are currently involved. Going deep into the principles, it starts by shedding light on the essence of hedgehog farming and examining its inherent appeal as well as the numerous advantages it offers. This book provides a strong basis for effective hedgehog husbandry by explaining common misconceptions and providing insight into hedgehog behavior.

The trip begins with vital information on choosing the best type of hedgehog and setting up a suitable farm, backed by necessary tools and thorough feeding and nutrition protocols. Stressing the importance of health and cleanliness guarantees that hedgehog welfare is maintained at all times.

The manual then delves into the nuances of caring for hedgehogs, covering everything from daily schedules to handling methods and health tracking.

It provides farmers with information on how to properly manage common health issues and establish grooming and washing practices.

Breeding is a crucial topic that is discussed in great detail, explaining breeding cycles, pairing up, giving birth, and caring for babies. The manual places a strong emphasis on ethical issues in genetic management as well as appropriate breeding techniques.

The topic of housing and enclosures is thoroughly examined, including several kinds of housing, building advice, enrichment techniques, and climate control methods for the safety and comfort of hedgehogs. Dietary considerations and nutritional demands are explained, guaranteeing balanced diets and taking unique dietary needs into account.

The comprehensive guide covers every aspect of health and wellness, including parasite control, veterinarian interventions, preventative care, and health sign recognition.

With this knowledge, farmers can better handle, comprehend, bond with, train, and control hedgehog hostility or fear.

The complexities of breeding are explained, including genetics, breeding tactics, moral behavior, and record-keeping. Farmers are guided through licensing, compliance, environmental issues, and inspection handling as legal and regulatory aspects is demystified.

All common questions and concerns are covered in detail, including how to handle aggression, health problems, escape prevention, breeding difficulties, and marketing tactics. This book offers a comprehensive strategy for successful hedgehog farming by combining knowledge with real-world experience.

CHAPTER ONE

INTRODUCTION TO HEDGEHOG FARMING

HEDGEHOG FARMING: WHAT IS IT?

Raising hedgehogs in a controlled environment for a variety of uses, including pets, educational initiatives, and conservation efforts, is known as "hedgehog farming." Ensuring their general well-being, giving appropriate nutrition, and establishing appropriate habitats are all part of the process. To provide an environment that will allow hedgehogs to flourish, novices in the field should concentrate on learning about the natural habitat, food requirements, and social habits of the species.

Learning about hedgehog care, such as housing demands, feeding regimens, and medical procedures, is a prerequisite to beginning hedgehog farming. This entails being knowledgeable about the temperaments and particular requirements of various hedgehog species, such as the African Pygmy hedgehog.

Beginners should also become acquainted with the laws and rules about the ownership of hedgehogs as pets or for business.

Animal lovers have a rare opportunity to support conservation efforts or participate in responsible pet ownership through hedgehog farming. It calls for commitment, tolerance, and a readiness to keep learning and refining techniques for providing care for these amazing animals. Beginners can have a fulfilling experience in hedgehog farming by adhering to recommended practices and getting advice from knowledgeable veterinarians or other hedgehog farmers.

WHY BEGIN A FARM FOR HEDGEHOGS?

For people who are enthusiastic about protecting and caring for animals, starting a hedgehog farm can be a rewarding endeavor. Interesting animals, hedgehogs have distinctive qualities that make them ideal as pets or educational ambassadors. One may support responsible pet ownership, advance hedgehog welfare, and inform the public about these intriguing creatures by starting a hedgehog farm.

Entrepreneurship opportunities are also provided by hedgehog farming. For example, one can responsibly raise hedgehogs to sell to pet owners or educational organizations. Hedgehog farms can also help with conservation efforts by working with wildlife rehabilitation facilities or taking part in breeding projects for endangered hedgehog species.

Hedgehog farming also gives people the chance to get hands-on experience with animal husbandry and pick up useful skills in diet planning, habitat maintenance, and medical procedures.

Seeing a hedgehog grow and develop under your care and sharing your knowledge and excitement with other people who are also fascinated by these endearing animals may be a fulfilling experience.

ADVANTAGES OF FARMING HEDGEHOGS

For people who care about animal welfare and conservation as well as communities, hedgehog farming has a lot to offer. One of the main advantages is the chance to encourage ethical pet keeping by giving families or individuals searching for unusual pets well-cared-for hedgehogs. This may raise awareness of the need for good hedgehog care and help lower the market for pets that are gathered from the wild.

Hedgehog farms can also act as educational institutions by providing information on habitat requirements, conservation issues, and hedgehog behavior. This educational outreach can increase awareness of hedgehogs and their importance to ecosystems while also serving as inspiration for conservation initiatives.

Hedgehog farming can help save hedgehog species, particularly those that are threatened in the wild, according to conservationists. Farms may help protect wildlife and conserve biodiversity by taking part in breeding programs and exchanging information about hedgehog conservation.

RECOGNIZING HEDGEHOG BEHAVIOR

Successful hedgehog farming requires an understanding of hedgehog behavior. Hedgehogs are nocturnal creatures with distinct social structures and habits. To protect the well-being of their hedgehogs, novices in hedgehog farming should get familiar with body language indicators, such as huffing or hissing when upset.

Hedgehog behavior has several important facets to take into account, including food choices, activity levels, and habitat needs. As insectivores, hedgehogs need a diet high in fiber and protein, along with occasional treats like fruits or vegetables.

Offering stimulating activities, such as exercise wheels or hiding places can encourage their innate behaviors and improve their mental and physical well-being.

Furthermore, group housing and breeding operations require a comprehension of hedgehog social habits. Although they are primarily solitary creatures, hedgehogs occasionally engage in territorial behavior, particularly when it comes to mating. Hedgehogs kept in captivity can live in peaceful environments by dividing up their living quarters and keeping an eye on interactions.

FREQUENTLY HELD MYTHS REGARDING HEDGEHOGS

Hedgehogs are popular pets and educational animals, but they're also the subject of many myths that may affect their welfare and upkeep. Because of the widespread belief that hedgehogs are low-maintenance pets, some owners fail to provide their hedgehogs with the right food, enrichment, and medical treatment.

To properly care for hedgehogs, newcomers to the hobby must be made aware of the dedication and accountability involved.

Another myth is that all types of hedgehogs are good for farming or as pets. Certain hedgehog species are more suited for domestication than others due to differences in their demands and temperaments. To guarantee the best possible care and well-being, novice farmers should investigate hedgehog species and select those that fit their farming objectives and skill level.

There are other myths regarding hedgehog behavior, like the idea that they can roll into a perfect ball at any time they sense danger. Hedgehogs do roll up entirely as a protective strategy; however, this may not always be the case, particularly if they feel at ease or are inquisitive about their surroundings. Beginners can avoid misconceptions regarding hedgehog behavior and give adequate care by being aware of these subtleties.

CHAPTER TWO

BEGINNING

SELECTING THE APPROPRIATE HEDGEHOG TYPE

Choosing the right species is essential when starting a hedgehog farm. The most frequent species for farming include the African pygmy hedgehog, the European hedgehog, and the Algerian hedgehog. Before selecting a decision, it is crucial to learn about and comprehend the distinctions between each species because they all have unique traits and needs. The African pygmy hedgehog is frequently suggested for novices because of its diminutive stature, kind disposition, and simplicity of care. But European hedgehogs are also well-liked because of their hardiness and climate adaptability.

Consider things like climatic compatibility, access to veterinary care, and local laws governing ownership of unusual pets before purchasing hedgehogs for your farm. To guarantee the health and genetic heritage of your hedgehogs, it is best to purchase them from reliable breeders or rescue organizations. It's important to follow quarantine guidelines and proper documentation to keep pathogens off your farm. Selecting the appropriate species of hedgehog will set you up for success in farming.

CREATING THE FARM ENVIRONMENT

The production and well-being of hedgehogs depend on the creation of an appropriate habitat for their farming. First, create an enclosure with plenty of room for natural behaviors and movement. To avoid congestion and territorial disputes, it is advised that each hedgehog have an enclosure that is at least four square feet in size. Make sure the enclosure has sturdy walls to keep out intruders and to keep predators out.

The bedding material ought to be easy to clean, absorbent, and non-toxic. Aspen shavings, paper-based bedding, and fleece liners are common choices. To promote both physical and mental activity, provide hiding places and enrichment materials like toys, wheels, and tunnels.

Controlling the temperature is essential since hedgehogs like warm environments that range from 72 to 80°F (22 to 27°C). To keep your home at the ideal temperature, especially in the winter, use heating pads or lights. Hedgehog health and hygiene depend on the farm environment being cleaned and maintained on a regular basis.

ESSENTIAL BASIC EQUIPMENT

It's essential to have the right materials and equipment for effective management and upkeep of your hedgehog farm. Begin with an appropriate enclosure, bedding, food and water bowls, and hiding spots. Purchase a high-quality heat source to keep the enclosure at the ideal temperature. Accurate temperature and humidity monitoring is aided by the use of a thermometer and hygrometer.

Hedgehogs should be fed a balanced diet that includes commercial hedgehog chow along with fresh produce, fruits, and occasionally prepared meats or insects for protein.

Using pet nail clippers, periodically trim their nails to avoid irritation and overgrowth. For unexpected situations, have a first aid kit stocked with basic materials like bandages, antiseptics, and wound care items. Having the necessary equipment on hand guarantees efficient operations and enhances the health of your hedgehog farm.

GUIDELINES FOR NUTRITION AND FEEDING

For the hedgehogs on your farm to remain healthy and vibrant, proper nourishment is essential. Provide a well-balanced meal with commercial hedgehog food as the main nutrient source. To make sure there is the right amount of protein, fat, and fiber, look for brands that are specially made for hedgehogs. For extra vitamins and minerals, include fresh fruits and vegetables in their diet, such as apples, carrots, and leafy greens.

Foods heavy in sugar, salt, or preservatives should not be given to hedgehogs as they can cause health issues. To stop dehydration, give clean, fresh water every day in a dish that won't spill.

To maintain a healthy weight, keep an eye on their food intake and make any necessary portion adjustments. To avoid contamination and bugs, clean food dishes frequently and get rid of any uneaten food. Adhering to these food and dietary recommendations can help your hedgehog farm stay healthy and long-lived.

HEALTH AND PERSONAL CARE ROUTINES

Ensuring the health and well-being of hedgehogs on your farm requires maintaining high standards of hygiene and health. Plan for routine veterinary examinations to keep an eye on your pet's health and quickly handle any issues. Immunizations, avoidance of parasites, and dental care are essential components of hedgehog health maintenance.

Maintain a tidy living space for them by routinely clearing out trash and wiping down surfaces. To avoid dangerous chemicals that could impair a hedgehog's health, use cleaning supplies that are safe for pets. Keep an eye out for symptoms of disease, such as tiredness, loss of appetite, or strange discharges, based on their behavior and looks. To stop the spread of disease, quarantine fresh hedgehogs before releasing them into the farm population. To react appropriately to medical crises, familiarize yourself with typical health conditions and emergency protocols about hedgehogs. You may establish a secure and productive environment for hedgehog farming by placing a high priority on health and hygiene procedures.

CHAPTER THREE

HEDGEHOG WELFARE

DAY-TO-DAY MAINTENANCE

Regular daily care is crucial for the well-being of hedgehogs when it comes to their maintenance. This regimen entails giving them clean, fresh food and drinks every day, keeping their enclosure clean regularly to preserve hygiene, and making sure they have a cozy and safe place to live. Since hedgehogs are nocturnal animals, the nighttime is when they eat and are most active. For them to thrive, it's critical to create a routine that complements their innate behavior.

Hedgehogs need to be fed a well-balanced diet that includes premium hedgehog food and sporadic treats like fruits or insects. It is imperative to keep an eye on their food consumption and modify portions as needed to avoid obesity or malnutrition. Hedgehogs require food and clean water at all times; the latter should ideally be supplied in a shallow dish that is convenient for them to reach and drink from.

Another essential part of their regular care is cleaning their enclosure. This entails cleaning dirty areas on a spot basis, changing bedding frequently, and sanitizing their living place to stop the growth of bacteria and smells. Providing toys, hiding places, and tunnels are examples of enrichment activities that might assist hedgehogs to stay cognitively active and avoid boredom. All things considered, a comprehensive daily care regimen guarantees that hedgehogs stay happy and healthy companions.

TREATING AND GETTING ALONG WITH HEDGEHOGS

A vital component of developing a relationship with these unusual pets is handling and socializing hedgehogs. Hedgehogs can be timid or defensive at first, but with time and kind care, they can learn to feel more at ease with people. It's important to approach them quietly and to stay away from loud noises or abrupt movements that can frighten them.

It's crucial to provide a hedgehog with adequate body support when touching them so they feel safe and at ease. Take them up from below with both hands; do not catch them by the tail or quills. Introduce handling sessions gradually, extending their length from brief beginnings to longer ones as they get used to being held.

Regular engagement with people outside of their enclosure allows hedgehogs to explore new areas and respond to a variety of stimuli, which is known as socialization. Building confidence and trust between hedgehogs and their owners can be facilitated by offering supervised playtime in a secure environment. But it's crucial to keep an eye on their conduct and keep them out of stressful or overstimulating environments.

Hedgehog owners may create enduring relationships with their pets and provide them with enriching experiences by taking the time to handle and socialize them gently and carefully.

KEEPING AN EYE ON WELL-BEING

A vital component of having a hedgehog as a pet is keeping an eye on its health and well-being. Frequent observation and health examinations can aid in the early detection of any illness or problems, enabling timely veterinarian care when required. Keeping an eye on their eating patterns, exercise levels, and general demeanor are important components of monitoring.

Hedgehogs in excellent health should be interested in their food and have a strong appetite. Any abrupt shifts in appetite or eating habits should be noticed and looked into further. Comparably, keeping an eye on their activity levels can reveal whether they are running on their wheel, burrowing, and exploring—all typical hedgehog activities.

You can also see any indicators of pain, discomfort, or anxiety by watching how they behave. Abnormal habits in hedgehogs, such as excessive scratching, self-anointing, or lethargy, may be a sign of underlying health problems. It's also crucial to routinely examine their skin, ears, nose, and eyes for any anomalies or indications of damage.

It is possible to guarantee that hedgehogs receive timely medical attention and preventive care by keeping correct health records and arranging routine veterinary check-ups. Proactively keeping an eye on their health and well-being is beneficial to their general health and pet's quality of life.

MANAGING TYPICAL HEALTH CONCERNS

Hedgehogs may have typical health problems that call for care and attention, just like any other pet. Hedgehog owners can provide their pets with the finest care possible if they are aware of these problems and know how to resolve them. Hedgehogs frequently suffer from respiratory infections, mites, obesity, dental disorders, and skin conditions.

Poor ventilation or being around drafts can cause respiratory infections, which can cause symptoms like wheezing, sneezing, or nasal discharge. Respiratory problems can be avoided by maintaining a clean workplace and enough ventilation. Another frequent issue that can irritate and itchy the skin is mites. If mites are suspected, regular skin inspection and veterinary consultation are required.

Overeating or inactivity can contribute to obesity, which can cause diabetes and other health concerns like joint problems. Hedgehog obesity can be avoided by giving them opportunities for physical exercise and by keeping an eye on their nutrition.

Dental issues can also arise and need to be treated by veterinarians, such as enlarged teeth or infections.

Dryness, flakiness, or hair loss on the skin could be signs of underlying medical conditions or poor skin care. Hedgehog health depends on maintaining good hygiene, feeding them balanced food, and taking care of any environmental issues causing skin issues. The management and treatment of common health disorders in hedgehogs depend heavily on routine veterinary check-ups and timely attention to any health concerns.

TIPS FOR BATHING AND GROOMING

Hedgehogs need special care and gentle handling during grooming and washing. Although hedgehogs are generally clean creatures who groom themselves frequently, they might need to take occasional showers to maintain the health of their skin and quills. It's critical to employ hedgehog-safe products and methods in order to prevent stress or skin irritation.

Use lukewarm water in a shallow container that fits the hedgehog's weight so they can stand comfortably without being completely submerged when giving them a bath. Human shampoos and soaps can be too strong for their delicate skin, so stay away from using them.

It is advised to give hedgehogs oatmeal showers or shampoos designed specifically for them to clean and soothe their skin.

Don't soak their face or ears; instead, only softly moisten their coat and quills throughout the bath. To gently scrub their quills and get rid of any dirt or debris, use a small animal grooming brush or a toothbrush with soft bristles. To make sure there is no soap residue left on their skin, properly rinse.

After bathing them, pat them dry with a gentle cloth and let them air dry fully in a warm, draft-free space. Hedgehogs can become stressed and have their skin dried off if they use hair dryers or high heat. Regular grooming should be a component of their care regimen to preserve their general health and well-being. This includes clipping their nails and looking for any indications of skin conditions or parasites.

CHAPTER FOUR

HEDGEHOG BREEDING

RECOGNIZING THE CYCLES OF HEDGEHOG BREEDING

Understanding the natural breeding cycles of hedgehogs, which are impacted by age, health, and environmental factors, is essential to successful breeding. Male hedgehogs, known as boars, mature sexually at roughly 8–10 months of age, while females, known as sows, usually attain sexual maturity at 6–8 months. Hedgehogs mate during the extended daylight hours of spring and summer, which means that these are their breeding seasons.

It is essential to observe hedgehog behavior and physical signs to properly breed them. Male hedgehogs may become more chatty and aggressive in their pursuit of females during the breeding season. Conversely, females may show receptiveness by bending their backs and letting the male get near.

Comprehending these indicators facilitates the efficient timing of the reproductive process.

Establishing an appropriate breeding habitat is also crucial. Encouraging effective reproductive habits requires providing a large, hygienic, stress-free enclosure with appropriate bedding, temperature control, and hiding places. This will imitate their native habitat.

HOW TO CHOOSE BREEDING PAIRS

An essential part of raising hedgehogs is choosing the appropriate breeding pairings. To guarantee healthy progeny entails evaluating the temperament, genetics, and general health of prospective breeding hedgehogs. To reduce the possibility of passing on undesirable qualities to the progeny, start by selecting hedgehogs that have no known hereditary disorders or genetic problems.

Take into account the hedgehogs' temperament; people who are too timid or aggressive could not be good parents.

Select for gregarious, inquisitive, and calm hedgehogs, as these characteristics are frequently transferred to their offspring. Furthermore, as older hedgehogs may have lower fertility or reproductive problems, find out about their age and reproductive history.

In order to prevent inbreeding and preserve a healthy hedgehog population, strive for genetic diversity when choosing breeding couples. Maintain thorough documentation of the breeding line and past offspring to monitor genetic characteristics and guide future pairing decisions.

PROCESS OF PREGNANCY AND DELIVERY

Upon the successful mating of breeding pairs, the female hedgehog begins her pregnancy, which normally lasts 35–40 days. Give the expectant sow a cozy nesting space during this period, furnished with fleece or shredded paper for soft bedding. Keep a watchful eye out for any indications of anxiety or health problems, such as hunger decrease or rapid weight gain.

The female may get increasingly agitated as the due date draws near and begin nesting activities, such as gathering bedding and moving her nest. Make sure the nesting place is warm, peaceful, and disturbance-free in advance of the birth. If additional warmth is required to keep the baby hedgehogs at a consistent temperature, give them some.

To reduce stress during the delivery process, try not to handle the mother or disturb the nest too much. After delivery, keep a watchful eye on the litter to make sure all of the infants are warm, healthy, and fed. If difficulties occur during or after delivery, seek veterinary assistance to protect the health of the mother and her young.

TAKING CARE OF HEDGEHOG BABIES

Hedgehogs, sometimes called hoglets after birth, are hairless, blind, and deaf from birth and are dependent on their mother for protection, warmth, and sustenance. For several weeks until the hoglets begin to grow more independent, the mother hedgehog will nurse them.

Maintain a consistent temperature range of 72-80°F (22-27°C) in the nesting place to facilitate the growth and development of the birds.

Giving the mother hedgehog a healthy food high in protein and vitamins can help her produce more milk and ensure the hoglets' wellbeing. To identify any problems early, track the hoglets' weight gain and general health daily. To acclimate the hoglets to human contact without stressing them out, handle them gently for short periods.

To promote weaning, provide the hoglets soft solid meals in addition to their mother's milk as they get bigger. Slowly introduce them to a well-balanced diet of premium commercial hedgehog chow, augmented with occasional treats, fruits, and vegetables. Keep a close eye on their development and seek advice from a veterinarian regarding their diet and general care.

GROWING AND WEANING YOUNG HEDGEHOGS

When hoglets begin to show interest in solid foods at the age of 3–4 weeks, the process of weaning them is initiated gradually. To help them start eating on their own, introduce soft, easily digested foods like baby food purees or moistened commercial hedgehog food. Throughout this transitional phase, keep an eye on their eating patterns and make any necessary diet adjustments to guarantee they are getting enough nutrients.

Give developing hedgehog pups a stimulating environment by providing enrichment items like tunnels, toys, and secure climbing frames. Handle the hoglets frequently and expose them to various sights, sounds, and smells to promote socialization and help them grow into self-assured, well-mannered animals.

Keep a watchful eye on their development and growth, marking significant events such as when their eyes open, when their quills expand, and when they become more mobile.

CHAPTER FIVE

RESIDENCES AND ENCLOSURES

HEDGEHOG HOUSING TYPES

There are several varieties of hedgehog housing to take into account, each with advantages and disadvantages. To begin with, wire cages offer adequate ventilation; yet, hedgehogs may find them uncomfortable as a result of tangled feet. Another option is plastic tubs, which can be easily customized and cleaned, but if they are not adapted properly, they may not have enough ventilation. Although they feel natural and offer insulation, wooden cages may need more upkeep to avoid degradation and mold.

Take into account the enclosure's dimensions as well. A cage that is at least four square feet in size is advised for hedgehogs since they require that amount of room to roam around comfortably. For more stimulation and enrichment, consider multi-level cages or cages with tunnels and hiding places for your hedgehog.

Finally, if you live in a climate that allows them, outdoor hutches are a possibility. Just make sure they are safe from predators and offer enough protection from the weather.

CONSTRUCTING A FITTING ENCLOSURE

Constructing a proper cage for hedgehogs demands careful thought and preparation. Start with selecting the appropriate components, such as wire mesh for ventilation and non-toxic wood or PVC for the structure. To protect your hedgehog from harm, make sure all of the edges are smooth. For easy cleaning and to safeguard their feet, the enclosure's floor should be sturdy.

Add elements such as a shallow dish for food and drink, an exercise wheel, and a hiding place. For added warmth and comfort, choose bedding made of fleece or paper. To stop escapes and keep other animals and pests out, install a tight-fitting lid or cover. The cage should be placed in a calm region away from drafts and direct sunshine.

PROVIDING EXERCISE AND ENRICHMENT

Being busy creatures, hedgehogs need both mental and physical stimulation. Add toys like balls or puzzles, as well as tunnels and climbing frames, to create an enriched environment. To keep kids interested, rotate toys frequently. Hedgehogs need an exercise wheel to achieve their recommended daily exercise; however, make sure the surface is sturdy to avoid foot injury.

Mix premium commercial hedgehog food with insects such as mealworms or crickets, and occasionally add fruits and vegetables to create a varied diet. Every day, provide clean water in a shallow dish that is convenient for them to reach. To avoid obesity, keep an eye on their weight and modify their food and exercise regimen accordingly.

CLIMATE CONTROL AND TEMPERATURE

Keeping the temperature at the proper level is essential for hedgehog health. Using a thermostat-controlled heat source, such as a ceramic heat emitter or heat pad, maintain the enclosure's temperature between 72 and 80°F (22 and 27°C). Heat lights should be avoided as they might dry up the air and burn people. Regularly check the temperature with a thermometer and make any necessary adjustments.

To keep the enclosure warm in colder climates, add extra bedding and insulation. On the other hand, to avoid overheating in warm locations, make sure there is enough ventilation and shade. Hedgehogs are sensitive to temperature changes, so keep them away from drafts and abrupt temperature changes.

SAFETY PROCEDURES FOR HOUSING HEDGEHOGS

When it comes to hedgehog housing, safety is crucial. Cedar and pine bedding should be avoided since they may be detrimental to the respiratory health of hedgehogs. To stop the growth of mold and germs, clean and disinfect the enclosure on a regular basis. Look out for any potential dangers, such as poisonous plants, unsecured cables, or sharp edges.

Maintain the enclosure's security to stop injuries or escapes. Regularly observe your hedgehog's behavior and health, keeping an eye out for any indications of disease or harm. Make sure your hedgehog has regular veterinary checkups and that you handle them properly to protect their safety and well-being.

CHAPTER SIX

DIET AND NUTRITION

HEDGEHOG FOOD REQUIREMENTS

For hedgehogs to be healthy and happy, it is important to understand their nutritional requirements. Because they are omnivores, hedgehogs consume both plant- and animal-based diets. High-quality commercial hedgehog food, which offers vital elements including protein, fiber, fat, and vitamins, should make up the majority of their diet. Furthermore, it's critical to provide a range of fresh fruits and vegetables to guarantee they receive a diet that is well-rounded.

Since hedgehogs eat worms, insects, and other small invertebrates in the wild, it is advantageous to include dried or live insects in their diet. Popular alternatives for hedgehogs are mealworms, crickets, and waxworms. But since these can be damaging to their health, it's imperative to avoid giving kids toxic or unhealthy foods like chocolate, coffee, onions, and grapes.

Another crucial component in preventing dehydration is always having access to clean, fresh water.

Regularly checking your hedgehog's weight, keeping an eye on their eating patterns, and making necessary adjustments are all part of making sure their nutritional needs are satisfied. A veterinarian who specializes in exotic pet care can offer invaluable advice on developing a healthy, well-balanced diet for your hedgehog. You may contribute to the well-being and longevity of your hedgehog by being aware of their nutritional requirements and giving them the right foods.

SUGGESTED MENU ITEMS AND SWEETS

Your hedgehog's general health and happiness depend on the foods and treats you give them. Given that commercial hedgehog food is designed to satisfy their dietary needs, it's a practical choice. Seek for brands that provide a well-balanced combination of fiber, vitamins, fat, and protein. Fresh fruits and vegetables like apples, carrots, and leafy greens can be added to their diet as a supplement, but it's crucial to introduce new foods gradually to prevent stomach distress.

Choose nutritious snacks such as mealworms, crickets, or little bits of cooked chicken or eggs. To avoid obesity and other health problems, these delicacies should be consumed in moderation. Refrain from offering fatty or sugary snacks as they can cause weight gain and dental issues. Giving your hedgehog snacks during playtime or training sessions can improve the relationship between you and your pet while stimulating their mind.

To keep them from getting bored and to make sure they get a range of nutrients, rotate their meals and treats regularly. To maintain a healthy weight, they should always keep an eye on their consumption and modify portion sizes accordingly.

You can maintain your hedgehog's happiness and contentment by providing it with healthy food and periodic treats.

FORMULATING WELL-CORE DIETS

Understanding your hedgehog's nutritional demands and providing a range of items to satisfy them are essential to creating a balanced diet for them. Begin with a foundation of premium commercial hedgehog food, which usually consists of a combination of fiber, protein, fat, and important vitamins and minerals. Add fresh produce to their diet, making sure to include foods that are healthy and suitable for hedgehogs.

To prevent upset stomachs, introduce new foods gradually and observe how they react to various foods. To sustain their energy levels and general health, it's critical to give them a diet that is balanced in terms of protein, fat, and carbs. Refrain from overindulging in sweets or high-fat foods as this might result in obesity and other health problems.

A veterinarian who specializes in exotic pet care may offer tailored advice on how to create a balanced meal plan for your hedgehog that takes into account its age, activity level, and overall health.

It will be easier to make sure they get the nutrients they require to flourish if you regularly assess and modify their diet as necessary. You may produce a balanced diet that supports your hedgehog's health with careful preparation and oversight.

FOOD SUPPLEMENTS FOR WELL-BEING

Dietary supplements, in addition to a well-balanced diet, can help to keep your hedgehog healthy. Supplementing hedgehogs with calcium and vitamin D3 can help maintain healthy bones and avoid metabolic bone disease. You can add these supplements to their food or water by following the directions on the label.

Another helpful supplement that can promote the health of a hedgehog's skin and coat is omega-3 fatty acids. Seek for vitamins made especially for small animals and adhere to the suggested dosage amounts. It's crucial to avoid over supplementing because hedgehogs may become ill from taking too much of several vitamins and minerals.

Before beginning any dietary supplements, it's imperative to speak with a veterinarian to make sure your hedgehog is a good fit and to figure out the right dosage. Frequent veterinary examinations can assist in tracking the general health of your hedgehog and identify any possible imbalances or shortages. You may encourage your hedgehog to lead a happy and healthy life by adding the right nutritional supplements to their daily regimen.

MANAGING PARTICULAR DIETARY NEEDS

Certain hedgehogs may require a particular diet because of their age, health issues, or dietary preferences. For example, due to changes in their metabolism and chewing capacity, older hedgehogs could need smaller servings or softer diets. Softer foods or a combination of wet and dry food may help hedgehogs with dental problems eat more easily.

To create a customized nutrition plan for your hedgehog, it is essential to collaborate closely with a veterinarian if it has any unique health conditions like obesity, diabetes, or allergies. This could entail choosing low-sugar or hypoallergenic foods, modifying portion sizes, and routinely checking their blood sugar and weight. Providing the right nutritional supplements and avoiding items that worsen their health can also aid in managing specific dietary needs.

Monitoring your hedgehog's nutritional requirements and general health regularly will help you spot any changes or issues early on. By making appropriate dietary and care routine adjustments, you can enhance their quality of life and avert future health problems. Your hedgehog will get the finest care if you take proactive measures to accommodate any particular nutritional needs.

CHAPTER SEVEN

WELL-BEING AND HEALTH

INDICATIONS OF A FIT HEDGEHOG

It is essential to recognize the indicators of good health when taking care of hedgehogs. A hedgehog in good health will display specific habits and physical characteristics. First, take note of how busy they are. A healthy hedgehog usually spends the night exploring its surroundings and acting silly. Additionally, they ought to be well-fed, eat their meals quickly, and show an interest in sweets or novel foods. A healthy hedgehog will also have lustrous, clean fur that is devoid of fleas, mites, and excessive shedding.

The weight and physical state of the hedgehog are further indicators of health. A hedgehog in good health should have a well-rounded body devoid of any obvious indications of bulging ribs or spine. They should have clear, bright eyes free of redness or discharge.

Additionally, watch how they behave when being handled; a hedgehog in good health will not be overly hostile or scared, but rather curious and aware.

Maintaining a clean environment, a balanced diet and regular observation of these indicators will help keep your hedgehog healthy and happy overall.

PREVENTIVE HEALTH CARE INTERVENTIONS

Hedgehogs need preventative healthcare practices to stay healthy and disease-free. Keeping your hedgehog's living space clean and sanitary is one of the most important things. This entails giving them new bedding, cleaning their cage or enclosure regularly, and making sure they have access to food and clean water. Their well-being also depends on keeping their habitat at the proper temperature and humidity levels.

Giving hedgehogs a healthy, varied meal that meets their nutritional needs is another crucial step. This consists of premium hedgehog chow mixed in with sporadic goodies like bananas or mealworms.

Foods heavy in sugar or fat should not be given to kids because they might cause obesity and dental difficulties, among other health problems.

Hedgehogs need to exercise frequently to keep healthy. Give them the chance to exercise and explore both inside and outside of their enclosure, using toys and equipment that are appropriate and safe. Finally, arranging routine examinations with a veterinarian skilled in hedgehog care can aid in the early detection and prevention of health problems.

IDENTIFYING AND TAKING CARE OF COMMON ILLNESSES

Hedgehogs are susceptible to common ailments that need to be identified and treated very quickly, even with precautionary steps taken. Obesity is a prevalent problem that is frequently brought on by overeating or inactivity. Excessive weight gain, mobility issues, and breathing issues are among the symptoms. Reduce their fat intake and boost the amount of time they spend exercising.

Dental issues including enlarged teeth or dental abscesses are another prevalent health concern. Drooling, unwillingness to eat, and pawing at the mouth are indicators of dental problems. Antibiotics for infections or the cutting of enlarged teeth may be part of the treatment.

Hedgehogs can also have fungal infections or mites on their skin. Itching, hair loss, and skin irritation are some of the symptoms. Usually, a veterinarian will prescribe topical drugs for treatment.

Another thing to be concerned about is respiratory infections, which can cause symptoms including wheezing, sneezing, and nasal discharge. Effective treatment of respiratory infections in pets requires prompt veterinary care using medications.

VETERINARY EXAMINATIONS AND CARE

Keeping your hedgehog healthy requires routine veterinary examinations. The veterinarian will evaluate your hedgehog's general health during these examinations, taking note of its weight, bodily condition, and any warning indications of any health problems. Additionally, they might conduct diagnostic procedures to check for parasites or underlying medical issues, such as blood or fecal checks.

In addition to regular examinations, get in touch with a veterinarian right away if your hedgehog exhibits any unusual changes in behavior, appetite, or physical characteristics. Prompt identification and management of health problems can greatly enhance results and save additional consequences.

Give the vet a thorough history of your hedgehog's nutrition, surroundings, and any symptoms you've noticed when you visit them. The veterinarian can diagnose a patient more accurately and suggest the best course of action with the use of this information.

IMMUNIZATIONS AND CONTROL OF PARASITES

The management of parasites and vaccinations are essential components of hedgehog health care.

Although hedgehogs do not need to be vaccinated against specific diseases like dogs or cats do, they might still benefit from such precautions.

Since hedgehogs are sensitive to both internal and external parasites such as mites, fleas, ticks, and worms, parasite control is crucial. Check your hedgehog frequently for symptoms of parasites, such as skin irritation, itching, or visible parasites on their skin or fur. For advice on the best ways to prevent and cure parasites, speak with your veterinarian.

Furthermore, keeping one's living space tidy and upholding proper hygiene can aid in the prevention of parasite infestations. Keep their food and drink bowls clean, wash their bedding, and clean and sanitize their cage or habitat on a regular basis.

You may contribute to ensuring your hedgehog's long-term health and well-being by being vigilant about preventative measures, routine veterinary care, and parasite management.

CHAPTER EIGHT

MANAGING AND CONDUCT

APPROPRIATE MANAGEMENT METHODS

Using the proper methods when working with hedgehogs is essential to protecting both the animal's health and safety. To begin, approach your hedgehog calmly and gently. Steer clear of abrupt movements or loud noises that can frighten them. If they are not yet used to human contact, pick them up with gloves or a tiny towel.

To keep your hedgehog from feeling uneasy, support their body with both hands once you have them in your possession. Refrain from excessively handling their quills since this may result in irritation. Instead, concentrate on treating them with gentleness and allowing them to investigate their environment at their leisure.

To stop the spread of bacteria, wash your hands both before and after handling your hedgehog.

Over time, regular handling will help your hedgehog get more accustomed to you, strengthening your bond with your spiny companion.

RECOGNIZING HEDGEHOG BEHAVIOR

It's essential to comprehend hedgehog behavior to match their needs and provide them with a proper environment. Being nocturnal animals, hedgehogs are most active at night. To replicate their natural habitat, provide them with a quiet, dark space during the day.

Since hedgehogs are solitary creatures by nature, it's critical to give them room and refrain from putting them with other hedgehogs until necessary for breeding. They are normally calm, but if they sense danger or fear, they may ball up. Give them space and time to get used to new situations or people. Respect their boundaries.

You may learn a lot about your hedgehog's health and well-being by watching how they behave. Keep an eye on their exercise routine, eating patterns, and any odd behaviors that might point to health problems.

Hedgehog happiness and health are positively correlated with the creation of a cozy and stress-free environment.

GROWING CLOSE TO YOUR HEDGEHOG

It takes patience and effort to develop a close friendship with your hedgehog. To begin with, spend some quiet, quality time with them every day to help them become accustomed to your fragrance and presence. During these bonding periods, give them goodies or their favorite meals to foster favorable associations.

Steer clear of pressuring them or handling them too much at first, as this might cause tension and discomfort. Rather, give your hedgehog the freedom to come to you when they're ready, and as they get more at ease, lengthen the time you spend together.

Your relationship can also be strengthened by giving your hedgehog regular attention, soft petting, and comforting conversation in a calming tone.

Maintain consistency in your contacts with them and give them a secure, stimulating atmosphere in which to grow.

ACTIVITIES FOR TRAINING AND ENRICHMENT

The physical and emotional health of your hedgehog can be improved by training and enrichment activities. Begin by teaching them basic commands, such as arriving when called or using a stick or finger for target practice.

To keep them from getting bored and to keep their minds active, provide them with a range of toys and accessories. Hedgehogs take pleasure in burrowing through tunnels, scaling buildings, and searching for food concealed in puzzle toys.

Playtime should be a frequent part of their everyday schedule to promote exercise and ward off obesity. Watch how they play with the toys and make sure they're safe and appropriate for hedgehogs.

CONTROLLING FEAR AND AGGRESSION

Hedgehogs can be aggressive and fearful, so managing them needs patience and behavioral awareness. When hedgehogs sense danger or fear, they may exhibit defensive behaviors including hissing, puffing up, or balling themselves into a ball.

Steer clear of abrupt movements or loud noises that can frighten them and make them protective. If they show signs of hostility, give them time and space to settle down.

Fear and hostility can be decreased with the aid of positive reinforcement and gradual desensitization. Treats or praise should be given for quiet, non-aggressive conduct to strengthen positive associations.

If your hedgehog exhibits persistent hostility or fear, speak with a veterinarian or knowledgeable owner to identify the underlying cause and create an appropriate management strategy.

CHAPTER NINE

GENETICS AND BREEDING

THE GENETICS OF HEDGEHOG PATTERNS AND COLORS

Breeders aiming to develop particular traits in their hedgehog progeny must comprehend the genetics of hedgehog hues and patterns. Numerous gene combinations dictate the numerous hues that hedgehogs can have, such as albino, chocolate, cinnamon, and more. For example, the albino trait is recessive, meaning that for offspring to exhibit it, both parents must possess the gene. Conversely, dominant hues, such as cinnamon, require only one parent to possess the gene for their kids to exhibit them.

Patterns with unique genetic rules include pinto, snowflake, and mask. For instance, a group of genes called the pinto pattern causes the body of a hedgehog to have white spots when pigmentation is suppressed. To choose mating couples with the necessary qualities, breeders who are interested in creating particular colors or patterns must be aware of these genetic principles. With this knowledge, they can adjust their breeding strategies to account for the possibility that specific traits will manifest in the progeny.

Breeders can produce genetically diverse and aesthetically pleasing hedgehog populations by examining the genetics of hedgehog colors and patterns. This knowledge also aids in preventing accidental breeding that could result in undesired traits or health problems in the progeny. Breeders can endeavor to produce hedgehogs with distinctive and appealing colorations and patterns by carefully selecting breeding pairings depending on their genetic composition.

BREEDING TECHNIQUES TO GET DESIRED FEATURES

For hedgehog farmers hoping to produce hedgehogs with certain qualities or characteristics, efficient breeding techniques are essential. Selective breeding, in which breeders deliberately pick parent hedgehogs with the desired traits and then breed them to pass those features on to the offspring, is one important breeding technique. To make educated breeding decisions, this method entails analyzing each hedgehog's genetic background, including its colors, patterns, health history, and temperament.

A different tactic is line breeding, which entails mating hedgehogs that are closely related in order to maximize the reinforcement of desired features and reduce the likelihood of introducing novel genetic variations. To avoid inbreeding and preserve genetic variation within the population, this strategy necessitates close observation. To increase general health and vigor, breeders can also introduce genetic diversity by outcrossing, which involves breeding hedgehogs from several lines or breeds.

Breeders can also identify carriers of particular genes or traits through genetic testing, which enables more accurate breeding decisions. Breeders can improve the quality of their hedgehog populations and generate offspring with consistent and desired features by combining these tactics with genetic knowledge.

HEALTH FACTORS TO CONSIDER IN BREEDING

In order to protect the health of parent hedgehogs and their young, breeding operations must prioritize maintaining the health of hedgehogs. Thorough health tests, including genetic testing for common hedgehog health conditions like Wobbly Hedgehog Syndrome (WHS) and hereditary susceptibilities to specific diseases, are essential before breeding. This aids in the identification of possible health hazards and enables breeders to choose hedgehogs that are suitable for breeding with knowledge.

Additionally crucial to the health of hedgehogs while breeding is proper nourishment. Providing a well-balanced, high-protein, vitamin- and mineral-rich food promotes reproductive health and guarantees the growth of healthy progeny. Furthermore, keeping breeding partners' surroundings tidy and stress-free enhances their general well-being and lowers their chance of developing health issues.

Preventive treatment and routine veterinarian examinations are essential components of health management in breeding operations. Hedgehog-experienced veterinarians should work with breeders to monitor reproductive health, do wellness exams, and quickly address any health issues.

Breeders can enhance the welfare of hedgehogs as a whole and enhance the quality of their populations by giving health considerations priority in breeding procedures.

ETHICAL GUIDELINES FOR BREEDING

Responsible hedgehog farming is based on ethical breeding methods, which also improve the welfare of hedgehogs kept in captivity. Ensuring appropriate housing and care for breeding pairs and their progeny is an essential component of ethical breeding.

Encouraging natural behaviors and cerebral stimulation, involves giving people enough room, improving their surroundings, and fostering interaction.

Genetic diversity and the avoidance of undesirable genetic characteristics should be the main goals of breeding. Conscientious breeders don't just concentrate on patterns or colors; they also value the temperament and general health of their hedgehogs. They also abstain from actions such as over-inbreeding, which can cause hereditary illnesses and other health issues in hedgehogs.

Honesty and transparency are fundamental components of ethical breeding. Breeders have a responsibility to accurately tell potential buyers about the genetic background, medical history, and care needs of their hedgehogs. This encourages responsible ownership and makes sure that hedgehog fans can make knowledgeable selections when buying hedgehogs.

Additionally, moral breeders take an active part in outreach and education initiatives aimed at raising public knowledge of the needs and welfare of hedgehogs. Breeders support the long-term sustainability and welfare of hedgehog populations kept in captivity by upholding moral breeding standards.

KEEPING TRACK OF BREEDING RECORDS

For hedgehog farming businesses to trace lineage, genetic features, health history, and breeding outcomes, breeding records must be managed effectively. Every hedgehog should have comprehensive records kept on file by breeders, including parentage, dates of birth, genetic test results, vaccination history, and any medical conditions or treatments received. Breeders can use this information to monitor the general well-being and caliber of their hedgehog populations as well as to make well-informed breeding decisions.

Data analysis and record-keeping can be made easier and more efficient by using databases or software created especially for breeding records. With the help of these technologies, breeders can create pedigrees, track breeding pairs and offspring, and properly arrange information. For accountability and openness, digital records can also be shared with veterinary specialists or potential purchasers with ease.

It is essential to update and evaluate breeding records on a regular basis in order to spot trends, track genetic diversity, and assess the effectiveness of breeding programs. This information can be used by breeders to modify their breeding plans, enhance healthcare procedures, and guarantee the long-term viability of their hedgehog breeding operations.

Breeders can promote ethical breeding practices within the community and improve the quality, health, and genetic variety of their hedgehog populations by placing a high priority on maintaining thorough and accurate breeding records.

CHAPTER TEN

REGULATORY AND LEGAL ASPECTS

PERMITS AND LICENSING FOR HEDGEHOG PRODUCTION

It's essential to comprehend the legal requirements before beginning a hedgehog farming operation. Permits and licensing are crucial for guaranteeing legal compliance and preserving a viable business. To begin with, a license is required to run a hedgehog farm. In order to complete this process, you must submit an application to the local wildlife or agriculture authorities. A thorough description of your farm, including the number of hedgehogs you plan to keep, the facilities you have for their care, and your experience with these creatures, is usually required in the application.

Depending on where you live, you could also require particular permits if your application is accepted. These permissions may have to do with zoning laws if your farm is located in a defined region, animal welfare, or the transportation of hedgehogs. To ensure compliance, it's critical to learn about and comprehend the particular standards in your area. Your farm may be forced to close if the required licenses and permits are not obtained, or you may be fined.

One of the legal requirements for raising hedgehogs is the regular renewal of licenses and permits. This guarantees that your farm will always adhere to the regulations set forth by the relevant authorities. It's critical to remember expiration dates and submit renewal applications on time if you want to prevent interruptions to your farming operations. You may start a hedgehog farming business that is both legitimate and viable by being proactive and knowledgeable about the needs for licenses and permits.

OBSERVANCE OF LAWS CONCERNING ANIMAL WELFARE

The treatment of hedgehogs and other animals on farms is governed by animal welfare legislation. Adherence to these regulations is not only mandated by law but also crucial for the welfare of your hedgehogs and the prestige of your farm. The provision of suitable shelter and care for hedgehogs is a fundamental component of animal welfare rules. This includes giving proper diet, keeping living circumstances clean and safe, and making sure pets have access to veterinary treatment when needed.

Furthermore, animal care laws must be followed when handling and transporting hedgehogs. This entails adhering to regulations for safe transportation and employing appropriate handling methods to reduce stress on the animals. To evaluate adherence to these requirements, veterinary authorities or animal welfare organizations may conduct routine inspections. It's critical to be informed about any modifications to animal welfare laws so that you can adapt your farming techniques appropriately.

Maintaining compliance requires that you and your employees become knowledgeable about requirements for animal welfare.

Ensuring that your farm operates ethically and legally can be achieved through training programs on correct care, handling, and welfare procedures for hedgehogs. You may enhance the public's perception of hedgehog farming and establish credibility with regulatory agencies by putting your hedgehogs' wellbeing first and abiding by animal welfare rules.

RULES REGARDING THE ENVIRONMENT

Environmental rules apply to hedgehog farming in addition to animal welfare concerns. The purpose of these laws is to reduce the harm that farming operations cause to the environment and natural areas. Waste management is one facet of environmental rules. Hedgehog waste, including bedding and excrement, must be disposed of properly to keep land and water sources uncontaminated.

Hedgehog farms also have to abide by rules for habitat preservation and land use. If your farm is situated in a region where endangered species or protected habitats exist, you might require additional permissions or limitations on specific agricultural methods. Adopting sustainable farming methods, such as reducing chemical use and utilizing renewable energy sources, can also help ensure that environmental standards are followed.

Regulatory compliance may necessitate ongoing environmental effect monitoring and reporting. This can entail recording waste management protocols, testing the quality of the soil and water, and putting policies in place to lessen any unfavorable effects of farming operations. Incorporating environmental stewardship into your hedgehog farming methods not only satisfies regulatory obligations but also advances sustainable agriculture and conservation initiatives.

MAINTAINING RECORDS AND DOCUMENTATION

In hedgehog farming, keeping correct records and paperwork is essential to regulatory compliance. This entails maintaining thorough records of all hedgehog purchases, births, deaths, and transfers. Every hedgehog must have a distinctive tag or microchip that is connected to its own record.

These documents facilitate the tracking of the hedgehogs' movements, health history, and ancestry on your farm.

Record-keeping also includes administering medications and providing veterinary care. Records of vaccines, treatments, and routine health examinations are necessary for regulatory inspections and health management of hedgehogs. This data not only certifies that the animals are being properly cared for, but also shows that animal welfare regulations are being followed.

For tax and auditing purposes, financial documents about hedgehog farming operations should also be kept. This covers sales revenue, feed and supply expenditures, veterinarian bills, and any other money-related transactions pertaining to the farm. Whether digitally or in physical files, keeping documents organized and stored methodically makes it easier to access and retrieve information during audits or inspections. In your hedgehog farming business, you show transparency and responsibility by placing a high priority on maintaining accurate records.

MANAGING AUDITS AND INSPECTIONS

Hedgehog farming regulations include audits and inspections on a regular basis. Governmental bodies, veterinary authorities, or animal welfare groups may carry out these inspections to evaluate adherence to industry standards and legal obligations. In order to manage inspections efficiently and guarantee a seamless procedure, preparation is essential.

Examine all applicable rules and guidelines before an audit or inspection to make sure your farm satisfies the requirements. To find any areas that might require improvement or correction, conduct internal audits or inspections. Proactively resolving any concerns can help avoid fines or unfavorable results from government inspections.

When an inspector comes to visit your farm, comply with their requests for access to all locations and work cooperatively with them. Be ready to respond to inquiries regarding environmental management, record-keeping methods, animal care guidelines, and farm practices. Make sure all records and paperwork are easily accessible for scrutiny throughout the process.

Make a note of any comments or suggestions the inspectors may have made after the inspection. To ensure continued compliance with rules, take fast action to address any found shortcomings or areas in need of improvement. Take advantage of the findings of the inspection to improve your farm's operations and show that you're dedicated to making hedgehog farming techniques better over time. You may guarantee the long-term viability and sustainability of your hedgehog farm by addressing inspections with openness, diligence, and a focus on compliance.

CHAPTER ELEVEN

FAQS & FREQUENTLY ASKED QUESTIONS

TAKING CARE OF ANGRY HEDGEHOGS

Understanding the behavior of aggressive hedgehogs is essential for managing them. Stress, anxiety, or a sense of threat can make hedgehogs aggressive. The first thing to do is to carefully and calmly approach them, being careful not to shock them with abrupt movements. To help them feel safe, handle them with confidence and gentleness by supporting their body and picking them up with both hands.

Give a hedgehog space and refrain from handling them until they calm down if they exhibit hostile behavior, such as hissing or puffing up. Reducing their stress levels can be achieved by creating secure and cozy surroundings with hiding places and comforting smells. Positive interactions and consistent handling can help decrease hostility and foster trust over time. Speaking with a veterinarian or a knowledgeable hedgehog owner can offer more tips and strategies for successfully managing hostile hedgehogs.

HANDLING CIRCULATORY INFECTIONS

Hedgehogs frequently suffer from respiratory infections, which call for quick medical attention. Sneezing, wheezing, nasal discharge, and difficulty breathing are among the symptoms. For an accurate diagnosis and treatment plan, speak with a veterinarian right away if you think your hedgehog may have a respiratory infection. Antibiotics and supportive care are frequently used in treatment to aid in the hedgehog's recovery.

Keep your hedgehog's habitat tidy and sanitary to avoid respiratory illnesses. Maintain a clean cage, bedding, and toys to reduce the amount of bacteria and allergens they come into contact with. Make sure their living area has enough ventilation, and keep drafts at bay. Keep a watchful eye on their behavior and health, since respiratory infections in hedgehogs can be treated more successfully with early identification and treatment.

PREVENTING HEDGEHOG ESCAPE

Hedgehog cage maintenance and planning must be done with great care to prevent escapes. To begin with, pick a safe cage that has no openings or gaps that a hedgehog could get into. To stop digging and make sure the cage is impenetrable from all sides, use a solid bottom. Check the enclosure periodically for any loose or damaged elements that can jeopardize its structural integrity.

To lessen the possibility of escape attempts due to stress or boredom, provide entertainment and enrichment within the enclosure. To keep children engaged both cognitively and physically, this includes hiding places, tunnels, and toys. If you let your hedgehog roam outside of its cage, keep an eye on their outdoor playtime and make sure the location is secure to prevent escapes. You may ensure your hedgehog's safety and security by taking preventative actions proactively and diligently.

BREEDING PROBLEMS AND SOLUTIONS

Hedgehog breeding has its problems, which call for meticulous thought and preparation. Before attempting to breed hedgehogs, it is crucial to learn about their genetic makeup, health risks, and moral breeding procedures. Only ethical breeding to enhance the wellbeing and general health of the hedgehog population should be carried out.

Managing pregnancies and births, selecting compatible partners, and providing the right care for the progeny are common breeding issues. Working with trustworthy breeders or specialists in hedgehog breeding is one of the solutions, as are doing extensive health examinations before breeding and giving pregnant hedgehogs and their young the right care and nourishment. Ethical breeding methods put the health of the hedgehogs first and work to prevent overcrowding or other health issues within the population.

MARKETING STRATEGIES AND HEDGEHOG SALES

Marketing techniques are used when selling hedgehogs to draw in potential customers and guarantee responsible ownership. Start by crafting interesting and educational entries that emphasize the breed, age, temperament, and maintenance needs of the hedgehog. Make use of high-quality images and videos to highlight their beauty and personality.

Make use of online resources like forums, social media, and classified ads to expand your pool of prospective customers. Give thorough details about the history, current health, and any particular needs your hedgehogs may have. Help and advice prospective owners so they can make sure they are ready to care for hedgehogs and can provide a good home for them.

You can advertise your hedgehogs for sale by networking with other hedgehog lovers, going to neighborhood gatherings or pet fairs, and forming alliances with respectable pet retailers.

www.ingramcontent.com/pod-product-compliance
Lightning Source LLC
Chambersburg PA
CBHW051908250726

48659CB00002B/543